Yokum Wood

ROBERT AUGUSTIN REGNIER

authorHOUSE®

AuthorHouse™
1663 Liberty Drive
Bloomington, IN 47403
www.authorhouse.com
Phone: 833-262-8899

Published by AuthorHouse 06/21/2022

ISBN: 978-1-6655-6132-7 (sc)
ISBN: 978-1-6655-6131-0 (hc)
ISBN: 978-1-6655-6134-1 (e)

Library of Congress Control Number: 2022910429

Print information available on the last page.

Any people depicted in stock imagery provided by Getty Images are models, and such images are being used for illustrative purposes only. Certain stock imagery © Getty Images.

Illustrations created by: William, Michael, Patnode

Special acknowledgement for Margaret Schwartz for her help in compiling this book.

This book is printed on acid-free paper.

Contents

A Cup of Joy

The things we say
The things we do
It's a lesson in life
For me and you
Feel the breeze
Blow through the night
Down a road that's long
A vision of starlight
Back when the game was played
And the winners were strong
A hundred days have passed
And the best were never wrong

An Uptick Of A Movie Flick

A powerful connection?
To ultimate control?
But let me take you
For a graceful stroll
Let me float
Like a butterfly
Like a delicate seed
Coming down from the sky
And I'll keep being
You know I will
And dream
On the morning still
Where the birds
Wake up to a new day
And the world will keep turning
As it may

Grab Your Senses, You'll Need Them
Down in the woods
We found the next faze
But did we?
Was it really there

Deep in the haze
Far beyond what is known
Mercy starts with justice
A child with a Teddy Bear
But mothers
Like fathers too
Of families growing anxious
Turn away from a mood that's blue

On A One Front War

Sheltering
From hostel gun fire
Got to get me a message out
Over the telegraph wire
"Save us"
"come and save us now"
"In a world seemed lost"
"We must never allow
"Bad"
"To conquer good"
"With bullets flying"
"You should"
"And to the point"
"Just come"
"To our rescue"
"Before dead we become"

Captured, But Only For a Moment

Women everywhere
Behind trees
Under rocks
As far as the eye sees
Women everywhere
Yes they are
In Hollywood
Behind every movie star
Women everywhere
On the sea
In sailing ships
Oh I wonder what could be
When women every where
Get together to say
That men everywhere
Have only games to play

How Can You Say Otherwise

With shovels and buckets
Rakes and hoes
And with courage
This is how the rescue goes
Trust me
When I say we'll keep digging
By us the brave
The willing
The ones
Who value life
In a world
Of violence and strife
Look!
A hand!
Now a leg!
So happy we've made our stand

An Owl? Or A Mason's Trowel

So tell me
How did you get the word out?
You didn't yell
Or even shout
Cry wolf
Or holler
You didn't even get
Hot under the collar
So now
That we've settled that
We must figure out
Where I'm at
And that is
Or maybe it's behind
A grizzle bear

MANY YEARS MANY TEARS

The boy in the mirror
Are you really seven?
The boy in the mirror
You've now jumped to eleven
The boy in the mirror
Confidence do you see?
The boy in the mirror
Yes I'm the one, It's me
The boy in the mirror
He must go on
The boy in the mirror
But shadows he's upon
And the boy in the mirror
Can this be?
That the boy in the mirror
Has become a man for all of us to see

Come Along And Sing A Song

Undeniably so
Is a moon glow
A river flow
When it's time to go
Exercise in a total gym
But only on a whim
Then there's Texas Slim
Who is related to Sally and Jim
There were peace talks
But out she walks
To color with colorful chalks
Pictures of bird flocks
So left behind
Was what we couldn't find
But let us define
Those who are kind

Safe, And That's What Counts

But I must
Lead the way
From lonely nights
To the beginning of a new day
And is it only me?
Who can take us there?
From lonely nights
To someplace where
Our world
Is brightened by the sun
It's all of us
And I hope I'm not the only one
Who has been lost
In a lonely night
But be us all
To find the strength to put up the fight

As I Don't Feel Left Out

In a world
Where brooks begin
I try to stay
There within
But is this?
The right place for me?
It just might
Be all we can see
But water
Will always flow
From mountain lakes
There I must go
To take
One simple drink
So Am I a simple man?
I hope that is what you think

TURNED BACK TO COMPLETE THE CIRCLE

Determined
Committed
To have my top hat
Fitted
To a head
That has gotten a little oversized
But why is it me
The one who always cries
Yes I'm off balance
And I can't seem to keep my shoes tied
Or my belt buckled
And before I've lied
About the sun
The strength of its rays
And the clouds under
Oh how I love those rolling greys

Poignant Is The Moment

She could hardly talk
Because of her weeping
Yes she cried
As time was creeping
Minute by minute
Hour by hour
But as she is
Pretty as a spring flower
Her beau Tommy
Is about to sail the sea
She is waving him goodbye
And on this day it is to be
Her time for weeping
Her tears she can't hide
Yes she cries as her beau Tommy
Sails on the high tide

THE LADY WITH THE MYSTIC SMILE

So you've left me
You've left me now
To survive?
I simply don't know how
Lonely days
Are in front of me
Oh girl
What future do I see
And as you
Flew away I cried
Many tears
And how I sighed
Over lonely days
That are to be
So now
That's all I see

Coming In Four Wheel Drive

The deadline
Came and went
Then to the bottom
I was sent
And it was quite a journey
To way down below
Because the bottom
Was a place I didn't want to go
But 'm here
And I got to say
I'll be back on top
Hopefully some day
But it's not going to be now
So I just got to hold on
And dream of horizons
Far and beyond

Funny Math

We're talking here
As we are now
About the farmer's blood
That is on the plow
And the words say
People unite
We're on the right the team
But we got to fight
In our chairs
And over the hill
As we look down the valley
We can't kill
Fear
Or bold lies
But we can smile
Though sunny skies

The World Is

I'm a lion
With teeth
I'm a shark
Beneath
The sea
And the plain
Open water
Sugar cane
But there's music
An earie sound
But the lion still has teeth
And there's a girl on the ground
And the earie music
In an open ear
So earie music?
Got to stand up and cheer

VISA VIE

Give me sweet
Time and color
Asking for one
Then the other
Eyes forward
With paint brush in hand
Is there more to come?
Yes I do understand
And there is to me
A window and a door
A mountain top
Where condors soar
So the bargain is
A seaside bottom dollar?
But to the change maker
Comes a stone a day in Mason's Holler

Pennywise Bird

Two sparrows?
For a penny?
But in my pocket
I ain't got any
So tonight
There will be no song
In the castle
No sing along
But if you send me
A free bird
A beautiful rhythm
And song will be heard
On the air
And through the trees
So hear the free bird sing
On a summer breeze

And There's Clothes On The Line

The tallest tree
Shining water
The morning star
This moment caught her
Standing tall
And singing a song
I heard her sing
Then I sang along
Looking out
At the steam train
The misty fog
The pouring rain
But the road
We travel is long
So we must sing in our carriage
A summer song

This Knowledge

We share
And as we walk
We see things that are
Bright like a star
As we color with white chalk
On a board
Black as coal
So see the things
That flies on wings
Into a dark soul
But how strong
Or very weak
Is a bough on a tree
A ship on the sea
Or the love we seek

THE VOtE IS In

Amy meadow Flower
Give me a little kiss
Right here on my lips
There you can't miss
Because you Amy Meadow Flower
Is the apple of my eye
True though these years
I love you as I'll try
To be with you
Your loving heart
Come over and see
When we do we'll never part
So Amy Meadow Flower
Dig in the garden dirt
Eat a sandwich for lunch
Then an apple for dessert

If It Takes All Night Long

Voices in the rain
The mist sings a song
Mysterious are the notes
But let us sing along
The women in the meadow
Dance around the May Pole
The flute and violin play
Vibrations from the soul
And I can hear you
I definitely can
And dream in magic
In this magical land
So if the sky
Stays full of stars
Stay by me please
Because true love will always be ours

Soft Pillow

The preacher likes the cold
In his warm socks
But his fiery words are kept
Behind keys and locks
And say he does
From an open book
Back to back live
Fortitude is what it took
So come to the wooden pew
Open your ears and eyes
Hear the words from his mouth
Aimed to where the raven flies
So I'll never forget seeing
The bumble bee on the flower
The color makes me smile
It's happiness by the hour

Throw The Dog A Bone

So am I in a dream?
Oh yes I am
And I'm dreaming about
Peanut butter and jam
And all types
Of silver and gold
The story is now
As I want it told
About the dreams
I have in my head
Sometimes the bad ones
Do I dread
But on my pillow
I will dream again
And when they will stop?
It will be when nine becomes ten

I'd Rather Be Swimming In The Sea

Three thousand miles
Is how far we'll go
Being the kids are sharp
With their leather jackets just so
But we lost our wit
On steamboat road
There was air in our tires
But our feet were cold
So Sha La La!
Alice is here
Full of song
And near
The star dust
Falling from the sky
Can we catch it?
Maybe, so let's just give it a try

Cover My Face with Paint

When I woke up this morning
My eyes were bright
And they were for you
As mine is blue
Blue like Bluebirds in flight
I got up on a horse
Because I ran out of gas
But I'll smile bright
Hoping it lights up your night
So just let me lay in the grass
So where she goes
I will follow
And let me be the one
To feel the rays of the sun
And chew your gum but don't swallow

I See This Fiery Thing

Fire!
I see in the ring
Oh the flames
Such a scary thing
Quickly
Got to put it out
The fire in the ring
And without a doubt
We must see
Past the fire storm
Oh I feel
A wind that's warm
And we hear
An earie sound
Of the roaring fire
Standing on unsteady ground

Skipping Down The Street

The sound of your hello
Puts me on my way
So play misty for me
The song sung by seaside bay
Riding through the hills
On a white horse
I feel the wind
And of course
It's twilight time again
In the after glow
And as I ride
Time is passing so slow
So chances are
Your dreams are mine
Through the night
To morning sunshine

Such A High Profile Sea Monster

They are all seeing him
As is me
The sea monster
As he rollicks in the sea
And he's a deep blue
As is the sea he's in
With a tail with spikes
He has on his back a tall fin
Then his eyes
Flashed
Oh they flashed so
As up against the waves he crashed
And from my tiny sailboat
May I may
Say how scared I am
Now sea monster please go

BE CAREFUL BECAUSE A DIME IS MORE THAN A NICKLE

Going in circles
Around I go
Moving a little closer
Close to moon glow
And you are
Magnet and steel
A summer song
A spinner's wheel
So here we go
Climbing the stairway
Step by step
We'll find the way
To touch
The morning sun
How deep are your feelings?
Am I your only one?

REFLECTIONS

Doing it?
Yes I'm doing it today
I sit quiet
Letting my words say
It maybe time
To climb to the mountain top
Look over and see
Hoping our dreams won't stop
Dreaming?
Because birds will fly
Children will sing
As clouds will grace the sky
So I'll look up
Because I want to see
The beautiful sunset
That's in front of me

WORTH FIGHTING FOR

Going it alone
When roses are red
When bluebirds sing
And sorrow is put to bed
But I'll travel on
A road very long
On my horse I sing
A happy traveling song
And to be
Climbing to a tomorrow
Again I don't like
Sadness and sorrow
So the frog climbed up
And jumped off a stone
I'm happy with my life
Don't ever want to be alone

Dust my Broom

Hi there and the mystery is solved
I've found the opposite of pink
Linda and Daniele
Told me what they think
It was tough
Minds were crashing
Gears were turning
In heads where they were meshing
You never know
What serious thoughts would bring
When minds come together
And bluebirds sing
So the mystery is solved
The answer can be seen
The opposite of pink
Is the color green

Loving A Woman Lost In Her Song

She started to dance
As the piano played
Her heels clicked
Her hips swayed
And with her hand in mine
We danced like up on
A soft cloud
There and beyond
So as
We danced
A feeling
Of beautiful romance
Came
Then I saw her erring's
How they laid against her shin so brown
Our eyes met
Quiet was the sound

LET'S TALK

Smart
But is this me?
I try
And my eyes are good and they see
A crazy world
And many things
So I just want to walk
And when the sparrow sings
I'm happy
My mind is in a good place
I see and I like
Your pretty face
We share words
We're two happy souls
Going forward we go
Towards our future goals

Eventually Your Time Will Come

Powerful
I take that from you
So I can't run
From a love I hope is true
I am me
And I'm looking for
Waves
Crashing to shore
The dark side
Of pleasure and pain?
It's not me
I like a spring rain
Kissed by a rose
A rose in bloom
So far away
From sadness and gloom

They Are Yours

Your eyes
See far away
See a sunny day
A spiritual way
Your eyes
Are soft and blue
They are the vision of you
They see what you do
Your eyes
Believe as one
Sight the barrel of a gun
See the rays of the sun
But your eyes
Are not like cold stone
They set a tone
They are yours alone

Something to Talk About

Snow and corn
And a house on top
Rocks that go west
Can't let the mind stop
Thinking about
The river below
A world going around
Flowers that grow
So breathe in
Three times a charm
And by then
Comes the red alarm
But the rocks
Are big stones pilled high?
Then I chose the name
Cherry Wild Sky

It Looks Normal, But Is It?

On a suicide mission?
Can't go on one of those
But I can hang out on the line
My well washed summer clothes
Because there's hope
The sun will come out tomorrow
So I can't get down
Or fill myself with sorrow
At least my summer clothes
Will be washed and put away
And a suicide mission?
Oh no not today
Just got to get out
My suntan lotion
And lay in the sun
Putting pleasure back in motion

Flowers Left and Right

Very still and quiet
But now I hear a lion roar
In the forest jungle
And above a vulture soar
So no longer still and quiet
As I see myself standing
For this
Is my understanding
That still and quiet
Can only be
Seen in a vision
In a dream I see
And I dream
Ever so
In the nighttime hours
And it is now so to sleep I must go

Never Settle For Tea In A Kettle

With the gift of sight
What did she see?
A vison of me?
Kneeling on her knee?
With the vision of sight
I can see you now
And this gift will allow
Me to see in the pasture a cow
With the gift of sight
I must look down
To flowers growing on the ground
And with this gift you'll never see me frown
And with this gift of sight
Where does it go from here?
To lose it do we fear?
But with this gift away from trouble we will steer

Waiting in a Vail

Must move in
Very carefully
To the girl with stars
Shining outwardly
From her eyes
Baby blue they are
But so carefully
Do I come from afar
And to you pretty girl
Can't move boldly
But like The sun
That shines only
With birds
Who fly in the sky
Look! She's come to me!
So no tears will I cry

Dancing on Air, So Do You Dare?

Whippoorwill
On the morning still
But will I will?
It only until?
A robin is a bird
Third base is the third
Then it occurred
Love is the word
Then there is this
Something that is
Like the morning mist
Your sweet kiss
So a pine needle is green
Sunbathers must be seen
The head of a college is a dean
And she was told she looked like a movie queen

A BLUE HAT

Step out
And dance
Circles in the snow
So let's go
And search for romance
I will
See a butterfly
Dance in the air
But there's no despair
In fighting the tears we cry
So in your pink gown
You can step high
And the band will play
As the clouds are grey
Against a blue sky

Smile As You Go

Your world
Never turns slow
And in a flower box
Flowers will grow
Thinking about you
With snow on the ground
Everybody says
Music is a sound
Fraught
By candy cane kisses
So come riding out
Because the cowboy misses
A lot of sleep
And glasses of beer
But his next sunrise
Is always near

CAN'T SEE THE BOTTOM

Down here
There's only one stop light
So catch me
Trying to break up a dog fight
I'm looking out
But not to far
Just got to drive
A special race car
And even if
I'm a thousand miles away
Your beautiful smile
I hope to see today
So looking across
I see the truth
But my head aches
Caus I got a loose tooth

A Fairy Tale Rules

Angel now
With silver wings
Eyes of crystal light
Her many many things
Bring joy
To this lonely heart
But darling I adore you
So let's never part
Ever
Or when the wind blows
Through the boughs
Of the apple tree that grows
So angel
Now tell me a story
Of beauty and grace
Stardust and glory

A Brand New Fool

Love has been
On my door knocking
Oh boy
It's been rocking
I took myself
To the end of a rainbow
Oh those Rock n Roll songs
Rock me so
Will the spot light?
See me today?
But I got a funny feeling
Love will find a way
To shake the stars
And make Rock n Roll dreams come true
Yes Rock n Roll dreams
Are for me and you

A Nice Conversation

I'm sitting in the gazebo
On this misty day
There's a stillness in the trees
A stillness that does say
Stay quiet
And just let time go by
So with a damp feeling in the air
And clouds in the sky
I went home
To start to write
Sometimes I worry
But I know everything will be alright
Because tomorrow
The sun may shine
Anyway
This day is mine

With Rain Drops Falling

Do you know?
The rings of a tree?
Count time
And rhyme
With nature in harmony
So where have all?
The young girls gone?
When will they learn
That's it's my turn
To be the one who's strong
And when she heard
The sparrows in the trees
She knew her name
Was the same
Mention of a Summer breeze

Dreaming All The Time

Stick around Mary Ann
The spider will weave
The devil will deceive
And we all will believe
In colors
Dancing on a rainbow
On beautiful flowers that grow
On little girl's dresses sown just so
So what we're doing
Is fighting hot with cold
With stories told
With words bold
So take this chance
To climb a steep hill
Dream through the night until
We see the morning still

NEAR THE FINISH LINE

Moon glow and shadow
And things I need
Dog and butterfly?
Johnny Appleseed?
And souls
From the past
Albatross on the sea
Crow's nest on a ship' mast
Up high
Sea gulls and hot air balloons
Airplanes that fly fast
Like ducks and loons
So you were right
You heard a song on the breeze
I heard it too
Dancing through the swaying trees

Take Me Back I'm On My Knees

The sound of your hello
Puts me on my way
So play misty for me
A song you sang on seaside bay
Ride through the hills
On a white horse
Oh I feel the wind
And of course
It's twilight time again
In the afterglow
I ride downtown
As time is passing so slow
But now
Your dreams are mine
Every night
To the morning sunshine

Got Something Out Of It

When I go low
Let me know
Time will tell
About coins in the wishing well
And only you
May never be blue
Then tell me why
There are stars in the sky
But in the movie Gold Finger
Will the stars linger?
It's coming up fast
But will it last?
The sun is in the sky above
And in it flies the dove
So I'm such a fool
Caus I fought the golden rule

But Here I Will Stay

Go where
You wanna go
So come on
You're now upon
A distant moon glow
So tell me
Am I right or wrong?
Do I cry?
Are there clouds in the sky?
Is there begging in a sad song?
But all there's left
Is what I can do
Like smell the flowers
Count the hours
Loving this sunny day with you

Simply Hold Hands

A word I say
The touch of my hand
An answer given
A lonely pail of sand
Is it a simple no?
Or an autumn leaf
A fleeting truth?
Or a strong belief
Once you think about
The gift of being strong
We say we can always
Sing together the winter song
Of snow and wind
Crows and Blue Jays
So in this season of peace
Let us not part ways

A Bit Of Mythology

John is a deer
And he sees with the cat's eyes
He warns " It's dark"
"And the raven will surprise"
Then he stops
With his heart pounding too
He says " Yes there's an end"
"And the song will always be true"
Look!
In the sky there's purple light!
But does it?
Make for a cosmic night?
But I am a deer
Which means I can run
I have brothers and sisters
And I have the sun

In The Woods

They run so fast
And they must keep running
Deer in the forest
Caus hunters are gunning
But no no no
Said the deer as they ran
The hunters say
But we'll keep shooting as we can
And deer are fast
They run run and so
Hunters hunt
But they are slow
So never have I've seen anything better
Than this chase
Hunters showing their power
Deer their grace

The Finishing Touch

Right or left?
Choose a hand
To salute
But make me understand
Why water
Always flows to the sea
And why trouble
Is there in front of me
So I walk
Where? Don't know
But water
Will always flow
With leaves
From Silvery Lake
And what a happy time
Time will make

What A Tomorrow Will Bring

Through a misty morning
There's the promise of today
And the hope of a tomorrow
To come our way
But I can't help from thinking
With snow on the ground
That more days like today
Are coming to us in our town
And there are we shouldn't change
There are paths we should walk
And radio songs keep playing
As stars shine in the dark
So let's talk about
The peacefulness of winter
Of days to come
Of a serenity that's inner

Words Written Long Ago

She sits down to write a letter
For once she was alone
Seasons change
On her desk was a stone
From magic garden
What will it make her say?
With thoughts swirling
She writes this today
"What will you do"
"If I say goodbye"
"But if I do I promise you"
"Blue will stay in the sky"
So two different people
One will write, one may cry
But words in the wind
Sometimes crumble and cry

A Table With A Light

A hat of stars
With feathers that say
The flowers are in the vase
And the clouds are grey
So don't take my money
And leave me penny poor
In the farm that everyone knew
Was a broken door
So I got to leave this planet
To go to a faraway star
Victoria with flowers?
In harmony? Yes we are
So five men look down
And see four working away
The clock keeps moving
But here we stay

THE ARTIST

Why?
No not now
He discovering white
But black will allow
Blue and red
Yellow and green
They're all on his pallet
But what does this mean?
So there's a need to keep
Everyone sure
Of color flowing
So will it endure?
Said the artist
In his hand his brush
Look! It's happening!
The picture and such

Do You Struggle To Fall Asleep?

So I chose to be in the dark
Because dark I am
And dark
Hits the mark
And do you believe me Sam?
Then I called
From the dark
Out openly
So sincerely
As in my life dark always hits the mark
But look!
Dark has gone away!
To the dark side of the moon
And very soon
I'll be in a beautiful sunny day

ALL OF US HERE COUNT DEER

And she cried
On the church grounds
And her tears fell
To the sounds
Of violins
And the piano player playing
A sad sad song
That was making
All who were there
Cry along too
Even though the day
Was in a sky of blue
And it didn't matter
Because there was no gladness
Just in air
So much sadness

THE LOVE NEAR YOU

Valuable Too?
Yes she loves a diamond ring
And when they sing
About a merry thing
The country I serve?
It's America here
A forest deer
A vista clear
Look at that!
We're headed for a celebration
A noble notion
A magic potion
So dollar for dollar
But only pennies there are
And far
Is a faraway star

It Goes Our Way

It's about to fall
I'm about to cry a tear
And night and day
Happens all year
It's been proven
Candle light will shine
And baby lambs
Will always be kind
Any concerns about the way?
The numbers add up?
But inspiration
Comes in a coffee cup
So like me
She's a quiet soul dreaming
Of castles in the sky
But there wizards are scheming

OR A LOT OF MILES

Is it time
To not stand still?
To sing with the Whippoorwill?
Or cop a thrill?
Pain will strike
But fish swim in the water
The book caught her
Saying my troubles are miner
Now modernize my chair
Because the springs are getting soft
But there are birds aloft
And we're coming off
A world
Where birds are singing
Faces are grinning
Losers are winning

Doors And Windows Open

Do I think I'm right?
But maybe I'm wrong
Now in the wind
I hear a summer song
And I hear you
My forever dear
And this summer song
Makes it clear
That water will keep flowing
And the sky above
May get between
Us and forever love
But the trees
With their leaves within
Will tell in their story
That our love will survive through thick or thin

Whatever, I'm Singing

All kinds of men
And women too
Dance night and day
To Moody Blue
I'll keep hanging on
And like you
My shoes dance
To Moody Blue
Fish and chicken
And lobster stew
Like to a clock we dance
To Moody Blue
Time goes quickly
And this thought is true
We must always dance
To Moody Blue

WITH THE CLOUDS WE SEE

What good is a night
That turns into day
But kiss me
In your special way
Please don't go
The wind is driving me down
But with it I hear
A piercing drumbeat sound
Driving rolling
And the beat goes on
To this new day
That we're upon
And a new beginning
The start of a new love
Is like the shining of light
From the stars above

Sitting Here Quietly

And I do
See a sunny day
And I do
Maybe see a way
To reach you
To make you mine
But there's the wind
And sunshine
That may come between hope
And endless love
But I'll try
And with the stars above
I have the feeling within
To make it all good
Our love
Be it be how it should

Lonely And Small

I remember Sundays
We would meet in the park
With pigeons on the ground
We would walk till dark
There was the sun
And you
A beautiful day
And a sky of blue
In the wonder of it all
We knew where we belong
We had us
We had our song
But like ashes of a fire
It all came to an end
The sun went down and I cried
Because I lost my Sunday friend

WORK WITH ME

Make it easy on yourself
Turn away from fire
Then with all your power
Climb a tower
Look! The situation is dire!
When candy
Sticks to your teeth
Beautiful brown eyes
Surprise
Me and all the others who are beneath
The shade tree
On the hill
And then
She came again
Saying I to cop a thrill

APPLE FAIR

Carnival thrill seekers
In the bright lights
A beautiful ballerina
In pink tights
But who can you see now?
And what has to be?
I'm just a man dreaming
Of sailing on the open sea
Oh yeah I must say
I'm not the boogie man
And to the beauty of all
We do what we can
So to the many
Good comes to those who wait
Crystal rain drops fall
On the magic garden gate

By My Count

I'm strong armed
And there's a feather in my hat
We're all watching
Are you worried about that?
People who are lost
Sometimes cry
But look I see ancient thunderbirds
In the sky they fly
And there's crazy low prices
Thank God I got a penny
Will it buy a diamond ring?
For my girl I want many
So the statement from the rabbit
Says I'm owning my decision
To hop and eat a carrot
Yes that's my mission

Keep It Going Straight And Flowing

Some people want
Shiny diamond rings
A bird that sings
Scary things
But time will be
As the world turns
The fire burns
Then the little girl learns
Not to be hurt
To just play a song
To bang a gong
Just try to be strong
So we all must live
Trying to stay
In a beautiful day
Dreaming about sailing away

Is It to Much To Ask?

He opened the door
He dusted off his car
I saw him walk
Then I saw clouds afar
Will it come?
Another day of sunshine?
Another you?
Or a deep gold mine
And gold
Riches beyond belief
But it's turning
Color on the leaf
So the sound of the jets in the sky
And all the things that are in front of me
Make me dream
Of what can be

What We Need Is An Apple Seed

Time
But where did it go?
When there's lips to press
And water to watch flow
You said you want to go for a ride
But will we learn?
To make love work?
Or to make the wheels turn
So maybe tomorrow
A breath we will take
Now my darling dear
I believe there's love to make
And we'll find what's missing
Hopefully today
To this
These words I will say

A Slower Pace Of Life

It was conceived
On a lazy walk
For then it came
This anticipated talk
"Agreed?"
"This is a sunny day?"
"Oh yes"
"One has come our way"
To my lazy walk
And then
For it
Came to me again
I felt it on my face
A soft breeze
I watched it flow
Through the leafless trees

Watch Again Then Count To Ten

Then the questioner
Asked a question
But what was
His suggestion
Was it that the moon?
Is made of cheese?
Can't rule it out
But now I feel a breeze
Because I'm not wearing a shirt
On my back
Yes a shirt
Is what I lack
But listen
I like saying yes
And how tall is the tall girl?
Very tall I guess

But The Word Was Heard

High?
Yes we're skyrocketing
But my knees
Look how they are knocking
Together?
And are we so?
But the sun is shining
That we know
And what answer?
Do you see?
Is it only that leaves in fall?
Turn colors on a tree?
Then against the wind
He fought hard
And when he cut the deck
He got the wild card

THE SCHOLAR MEETS THE GARBAGE MAN

Over there
Over where?
Yes over there
Is a grizzle bear
But over here
It's clear
That here in the forest
Lives a deer
Such clarity
In these words that say
For me
There is no other way
To look up at night
And count the stars
While eating
Chocolate bars

LEPRECHAUNS DOING THEIR THING

They are giving it a good
Going over
For the leprechauns
Are dancing in the clover
A couple of feet in
The others in the air
And where is this happening?
In the clover, that's where
Yes the clover
With leaves of green
The place where they all
Wanted to be seen
Yes they gave
A good going over
As they danced
In the field of clover

As The Sound Builds In The Valley

This is
A feeling of certainty
But only momentarily
Will I lean in intently
But that was yesterday
A day that's gone
Will there be?
A tomorrow song?
Please
Let me sing one now
And I hope
They will allow
But who are they?
A gang of three?
Oh what
Has come over me

BUT DONALD DUCK CAN SELL YOUR HOME

The camera saw it grow
The iron flower
Listen, At 3 Am
It's confusion by the hour
And pounds and pounds of bacon
Must be cooked well
Oh look! I'm getting older!
As far as I can tell
And it's hard
Why did they say it was easy?
But all I know
Is my stomach feels a little queasy
Maybe because I swallowed
A dollar bill
Wanting to be richer
Just a little richer still

I Love You As It Keeps Getting Better

Sixty Six?
Or seventy three?
But I must have sugar
In my cup of tea
And zero
Is less than one
Now take me
On a rocket ship to the sun
And yes
The sun is beating down
In my head there's Rock n Roll
I've heard it in Swing Town
And the beat
Keeps driving along
Oh how I love
A Rock n Roll song

Science Transformed

A result?
Or is it just what we can
But no no no
Just let me be a man
And if you want too
You can be a girl
And water down a drain?
Just let it swirl
But water down a river
That water flows
To the sea
This is how the story goes
And as it goes on
My head will stay in a cloud
And the baby in the crib?
She's crying out loud

Complete? But I Can't Stop Moving

Update your floors
For walking
Update your doors
For closing
Your windows?
Through which you must see
A wide wide world
That can only be
But for who?
Only the ones?
Who ponder
And deliver in tons
The answers
Then there will be no need for fire
Or wind
Just internal desire

But A New Thing Is Coming

A knew a man
Who failed as a farmer
And his wife
Wasn't much of a charmer
Their dog?
Boy he barked a lot
They tried to think of
Something they had got
Was it a can of corn?
A loaf of bread?
Something else?
What more can be said
Only
That the lonely
Solely
Can also be a phony

Let Them Fall

Dropping trees all day
Look how strong I am
Down they fall
Now I'll call
My good old friend tree cutting Sam
To cut and drop
Trees in the sun
And more will fall
Boy how they are tall
Got to get more tree dropping done
So to drop trees
Is something we must do
All day long
As we sing a song
So let me drop a tree for you

It's So Easy To Eat Apple Sauce

Of all I got
Of all we are getting
Think of all the pins
The bowling pin machine is setting
Then it pays
To find way
To turn black
Into a soft kind of grey
Now call your doctor
Make a stand
It's your body
He'll understand
If he doesn't
Turn on Apple TV
Spin the dial
To see what you can see

CLIMBING MY WAY BACK TO THE WORLD

The lights are still on
Overhead planes are flying
But they're still bombing over there
So there's a need for crying
Red Sox?
It's early they say
I look up
And see clouds of grey
So happy to see
Squirrels dancing
On the grass
Look how they're prancing
So I wonder
What this day will bring
A million dollars?
Or another song to sing

A Simple Day Is On It's Way

You decide
What's next
A pot of gold?
Or a witches' hex
And do it
As soon as you can
Yes you must be
A big man
Or a big girl
If that's who you are
But I don't think
Even a superstar
Could decide
What's next
A pot of gold?
Or a witches' hex

THREE, YOU MUST SEE

Come on Grandma
I can't keep standing in the sun
Or keep carrying the weight
Oh it weighs a ton
Sauerkraut?
Is that what I heard you say?
But on this park bench
It's clearly a sunny day
Now pick up the pace
You're talking to slow
And of a bow and arrow?
I'll take the bow
And I saw a turtle in a tree
But how did he climb?
Good!
I've found an end to my rhyme!

So Much Walk But Not Enough Talk

For those
Who pick a rose
You must close
The nostril of your nose
But flowing in
Is something thin
In a bin
Built from sin
Then there's an ocean
Put in motion
By a magic potion
And calamine lotion
So there's a leaf of green
Dancing with a jelly bean
A college dean
But there's always a good place to be seen

With Direct Commentary

A thin line
Drawn
Between here and there
And the morning dawn
And the leader is
Coming from the sun
But is he?
And does he want to get it done?
Maybe
And it all could be a joke
Then from a sleep
He awoke
Yelling
"Now what do I do"
"I hoping to see"
"A sky of blue"

Do It With Electric Innovation

The wind?
No a summer breeze
Flowers?
No swaying tall trees
I jumped in
Boy the water was cold
I hollered
Stating something bold
But what's this?
Little green men?
Oh yes
And they counted to ten
From their flying saucer they got out
"Look! We're Here!"
They did shout

LEPRECHAUNS DOING THEIR THING

They gave it a good
Going over
For the leprechauns
Are dancing in the clover
Many feet in
Others in the air
And where is this happening?
In the clover, that's where
Yes the clover
With leaves of green
A place where all
Leprechauns want to be seen
And they gave it
A good going over
As they danced
In the field of clover

THE SCHOLAR MEETS THE GARBAGE MAN

Over there
Over where?
Yes over there
Is a grizzle bear
But over here
It's clear
In this forest
Lives a deer
Such clarity
In these words that say
For me
There's no other way
To look up at night
And count the stars
While eating
Chocolate bars

But Donald Duck Can Sell Your Home

The camera saw it grow
The iron flower
Listen, at three AM
It's confusion by the hour
And pounds and pounds of bacon
Must be cooked well
Oh look, I'm getting older
As far as I can tell
And it's hard
Why did they say it was easy?
But all I know
Is that my stomach feels a little queasy
Maybe because I swallowed
A dollar bill
Wanting to be richer
Just a little richer still

As The Sound Builds In The Valley

This is
A feeling of certainty
But only momentarily
Will I lean in intently
But that was yesterday
A day that's gone
Will there be?
A tomorrow song?
Please
Let me sing one now
Something I hope
They will allow
And who are they?
A gang of three?
Oh what
Has come over me

Green Springtime Words

Sixty Six?
Or seventy three?
But I must have sugar
In my cup of tea
And zero
Is less than one
Now take me
On a rocket ship to the sun
And yes
The sun is hot
But I'm thinking
Of what I got
And it's Rock n Roll
The beat keeps me moving along
Oh how I love
A Rock n roll song

Watch Again Then Count To Ten

Then the questioner
Asked a question
But what was?
His suggestion?
Is it that the moon?
Is made of cheese?
Can't rule it out
But now I feel a breeze
Because I'm not wearing
A shirt on my back
Yes a shirt
Is what I lack
But listen
I like saying the word yes
And how tall is the tall girl?
Very tall I guess

HELP? BUT SHE DOESN'T NEED IT

She was digging
But slowly
With her hands
But only
The dirt
That buried her man
She can't bring him back to life
But she can
Still dig
To find the ring
She gave him
It was the only thing
That they didn't
Give her when
They buried him
So in the dirt she digs again

Dreams Of Spring Flowers

Snow snow
Go away go away
I'm tired of you
I must say
May the sun
Melt your whiteness
With its heat
Its brightness
And snow covers
A frozen ground
But now
I'm tired of you being around
You were nice
On Christmas Day
But now
Please go away

Witch Of The Roses

So dark
In many ways
The witch of the roses
In her garden she stays
She looks
Then with her wicked hand
Touches another rose
But there are those who don't understand
That a dark witch with beauty
Can still be
A witch of the roses
Now let us see
In your garden
How your roses grow
But witch of the roses
Dark you are we know

I Pulled It Out Of The Fire

All the sirens
Are all the same
Such noise they make
Must be described as lame
Lame?
Yes her left leg was bad
Which made her limp a little
So here's a cane, aren't you glad?
To be helped
To stroll through the clover
But before
This story is over
We must fry
Some eggs in a pan
Now laugh
As hard as you can

Our Seat At The Table

The truth teller's time
It's definitely now
With words like this
"The world is a field and you are a farmer's plow"
Now with your mind
Turn over the dirt
For this
It's time to sound an alert
Good
Now that it is done
The dirt is turned and the word is out
Now flowers can grow in the sun
And you and I
Can now go hand and hand
Gazing into each other's eyes
Strolling across this beautiful land

No Better Evidence That She's Dense

But?
As well?
Oh yes
As far as I can tell
But what she has announced
Is so much more
Than a thousands condors
Ready to soar
Particularly
For those
Coming up from behind
Is there a rose?
Yes there is one over there
Growing very high
So reach up
To a welcoming sky

Take Love Off A Shelf

When does it begin?
There has to be a start
We can't risk
Another broken heart
Is it by eating?
An apple under a tree?
Or is it by sailing
A boat on the sea
Look!
It may be in a meadow!
Or at night
Behind a dark shadow
So it's an old love
With a new start
And we can't risk
Another broken heart

THis is what a happening is

I love you
Caus you keep getting better
I'll say this truly
And send it to you in a letter
And these words
Are sent through the air
With a passionate kiss
Going from here to there
Yes we live
In different towns
But we got hope
Not frowns
Just smiles
And a way forward that is
Oh how I miss
Your sweet kiss

A Simple Day Is On It's Way

You decide
What's next
A pot of gold?
Or a witches' hex
And do it
As soon as you can
Yes silly
Be a big man
Or a big girl
If that's who you are
But I don't think
Even a superstar
Could decide
What's next
A pot of gold?
Or a witches' hex

Talk About What Ever You Want

So I grow all
My vegetables and fruit
After that
I give my flute a toot
Then I comb my hair
Parting it to the right
It is grey
But isn't out of sight?
But at least
For awhile
There is still
A crocodile
In the swamp but oh no!
Off my foot he bit!
So now I can't stand
But luckily I can still sit

A Seemingly Endless Cycle

But I want to cry
So just let me so
Let my tears flow
As on my way I go
And I'll cry
Helplessly now
And I can't allow
My mind to plow
Into a dark
Valley of hurt
Now I must sound the alert
Even though I'm stronger than dirt
Now take me
To a place over there
But is it where?
About true love about which we will always care

Neighbor To Neighbor

Thank you for the brownie
That was very nice
Not only must I thank you once
I will thank you twice
I ate it
After my lunch
Again
Thank you very much
For I say it
So sincerely
That your brownie
Was clearly
The best thing
To happen to me today
So let me thank you again
In a personal way

Supply Lines Defines Stop Signs

Well they got a pill
For just about everything
But still
I feel a chill
Every time I feel the urge to sing
But we're going to keep moving
Even if stuck in cement
And food and water
Are needed by my daughter
But I can't help with even a cent
So private citizens are behind
Those who are for sale
But they'll never take action
Or get any type of traction
Though they all know how to fill a pail

Otherwise, How Was The Play Mary?

Somebody
Is going to hurt someone
Will it be in the shade?
Or in the sun?
And how?
Will that hurt go?
Will it be fast?
Or excruciatingly slow
Excellent questions
With a simple answer or two
Or three
Remember, truth is always true
Then at last
That hurt will go away
Like a stormy night
Will turn into a calm sunny day

And She's Fighting Back Bravely

After an apparent
Lack of surprise
Again he hurt her
Again she cries
This time her tears
Fell on the bed
They shared
And only after these hurtful words he said
"I don't love you now"
"So I must go away"
"These"
"Are the words I say"
Then she said
"Just go"
"Don't make me cry anymore"
"I must now start anew"
"So just go out the door"

Words I Impose Upon

Do you see the bear?
Hopefully you do, hopefully you care
For the bear
So now you must stare
The bear down
As you hold your ground
And the bear may run
Directly into the sun
Past the flowers
But as you pass the hours
You must stop caring about the bear
You now must care
For the cow
Because now
You may need a glass of milk
As you wear a shirt of silk

A Man Of Wisdom In A Thunder Storm

Forget about meat
And the stars above
Water in a glass
Forever love
The dance of dances
Around the May Pole
Yes for me
It has all taken a toll
So I see one way out
It's to get the best deal
And the Universe
Is the only thing that maybe real
Other than another
Day of sunshine
If so for me
That'll have to be fine

The Highway To hell Is Being Repaved

Two?
For one low price?
WOW!
That'll be nice
Three apples?
In one hand?
How does that happen?
I don't understand
But with you by myside
We can go just about anywhere
But in a long dark shadow
Stands a grizzle bear
Growling
Because he wants some honey
Then she tickled his behind
Don't you think that's funny?

For Al I Know It May Be Time To Go

Mossing over?
To drop a weight?
Or to swing?
A garden gate?
But the wind
Is blowing strong
As is
A robin singing his song
And what's this?
Something white?
Or yellow?
No it's a paper kite
And with my hands on the string
It will fly above
And nothing can stop
Our forever love

Our Seat At The Table

Is it the truth teller's time?
Yes and it's definitely now
With words like this
"The world is a field and you are a farmer's plow"
Now you must
Turn over the dirt
For this
Is the time to sound an alert
Good
Now that is done
The dirt is turned and the word is out
Now flowers can grow in the sun
And you and I
Can now go hand and hand
Gazing into each other's eyes
Strolling across this beautiful land

A Pledge And A Promise

Lady Jane
Give me your hand
For me you are
Like the morning star
May we stroll across this beautiful land
Lady Jane
Our time is now
And this rose is for you
As is this sky of blue
Our budding love must allow
Us to shelter
From a spring rain
So with rain drops falling
And out my heart is calling
How much I love Lady Jane

I Pulled It Out Of The Fire

All the sirens
Are all the same
Such a racket they make
Is it beautiful or lame?
Lame?
Yes her left leg was bad
Which made her limp a little
So here's a cane, aren't you glad?
To be helped
To stroll across the clover
But before
This story is over
We must fry
Some eggs in a pan
Now you can laugh
As hard as you can

For All Part Time Human Beings

So I grow all
My vegetables and fruit
After that
I always give my flute a toot
Then I comb my hair
Parting it to the right
Doesn't it look good?
It's grey but it's out of sight
But at least
For a awhile
There is still
A crocodile
In the swamp but oh no!
Off my foot he bit!
So now I can't stand
But luckily I can still sit

No Better Evidence That Says He's Dense

But?
As well?
Oh yes
As far as I can tell
And what she contemplates
Is so much more
Than a thousand condors
Ready to soar
And particularly
For those
Coming up from behind
Will they find the rose?
It's over there
Growing high
So reach up
To a welcoming sky

Doors

I dream of doors
That open to the sky
I turn the knobs
Then I wonder why
Doors open
Then close again
And doors with light
That brightly send
Me to a gate
And through to the other side
Where the threshold lives
With the ocean tide
And tomorrow will say
Many things sweet
So open a door to glory
To a room where spirits meet

Hi, I'm your Forever Friend

I'm Mr. Blue
Can I talk to you?
About nuclear fission
A moon landing mission
Dumb things like that
Like where the queen sat
But I'm Mr. Blue
And yes my love is true
And I can give it
To you and sit
In a rocking chair
A happy place where
My thoughts can flow
And my feelings for you can grow
So I'm bring this poem to a happy end
Because you are my forever friend

His Is Me, Take It As It Is

Two nights ago
There was one
Two nights ago
I waited for the sun
And when it came up
I cried
Oh I cried so
Because for you I tried
Tried to get
Just a piece of your love
Then two nights ago
I cried again
And I cried so much
Because I couldn't get you gaze
Or from your hand even your touch

Safe From The Sound Of Shelling

Burning people's eyes
Is it the sun?
What is being done?
Is God the one?
I suspect
It can be more than this
That what is
For me your sweet kiss
And the children are
Safe for now
But how?
Can we allow?
What was left behind
A little piece of love
Or something of
More coming from above

Memories That Were Before

Lovely lemons
Apples of red
And I love dandelions
And roses in a rose bed
And after batting practice
I struck out
Oh, about ice cream
I had to shout
YA HOO!
A bat on a ball?
But strike one
Was the umpires call
And through the years
Don't bother counting the days
Then listen to Jimi play
His song " Purple Haze"

Watch Me Walk Briskly

Then came
A crayon from the same
Crayon box
But keys and locks
Weren't needed
After the garden was weeded
And weeds are green
Then the skunk was seen
And smelt
And his fur was felt
By her hand
But I don't understand
Why this was done
It didn't seem to be fun
No fun at all
But the horse is in the horse stall

Birds Singing Everywhere

Funny you believe
That way
That true love
Can only come today
Only do you believe
That this can be that
That one cookie
Will never make you fat
Then do you believe
That crows go caw
That a spaceship
Is what we saw
So believe what you believe
We are the crew
Being us
Believing it all to be true

PLEASANT DAYS IN THE GARDEN

I grow
Pretty flowers
They grow high
And they touch the sky
I watch them grow by the hours
Red and yellow
Purple and green
Are my flowers
Yes they grow by the hours
Pretty as they are being seen
So please look
To each flower
As many are there
And this is where
We come to feel their power

Of Course A Show Of Force

What more?
Do you know?
For why
Does the wind blow
It's the morning
And the sun is coming up
Hot coffee
Is in the coffee cup
An important time
To be alive
And home
There are words to drive
That said
Yesterday I bought some bread
To which myself I feed
After I got myself out of bed

She Is Clearly In Charge

With her hands
She clawed away
Desperately
Trying as she may
To grasp
To hold on
To the power
There and beyond
And with
Stars in her eyes
And with the big picture in focus
There was no surprise
That she made it
Her goal to get to the top
But that wasn't enough
Because for his love she couldn't stop

An Image To Hide Behind

Thank you
For letting me know
Now I can relax
And watch the flowers grow
Water them
And weed the weeds
Tend
To all their needs
Aren't they pretty?
Do you think it is so?
If you agree
You and I can watch the flowers grow
With a sun shining down
Such a pleasant thing to do
A great way to be together
For me and you

Pretty Clear, Pretty Blunt

The way
She got her name
Was to dream easy
Then easy it came
Winner it was
Of games played
For high
Her expectations weighed
And they came up
Very strong
A strong woman?
Yes as she came along
To play
An she played well
The game with me
A joyful story that I must tell

Watch Me Walk Briskly

Then came
Crayons from the same
Crayon box
But keys and locks
Were not needed
After the garden was weeded
And weeds are green
Then a skunk was seen
And smelt
And his fur was felt
By her hand
But I don't understand
Why this was done
It didn't seem to be fun
No fun at all
But she put her horse in the horse stall

Memories That Were Before

Lovely lemons
Apples of red
And I love dandelions
And roses in a rose bed
Then after batting practice
I struck out
Oh, about ice cream?
I had to holler and shout
YA HOO!
A bat on the ball?
But strike one
Was the umpires call
And through the years
Don't bother counting the days
Then hear Jimi Sing and play
His song " Purple Haze"

It's Me, Take It As It Is

Two nights ago
There was one
Two nights ago
I waited for the sun
And when it came up
I cried
Oh I cried so
Because for you I tried
Tried to get
Just a piece of your love
Then two nights ago
With a moon above
I cried again
And I cried so much
Because I couldn't get you gaze
Or from your hand even your touch

Birds Are Singing Everywhere

Funny you believe
That way
That true love
Can only come today
Only do you believe
That this can be that
That one cookie
Will never get you fat
Then do you believe
That crows go caw
That a spaceship
Was what we saw
So believe what you believe
We are the crew
Being us
Believing it all to be true

Not Needed Legal Reasoning

It's exciting
Even wonderful
When Sally
Carried a pail full
Of sand
To you not a thrill
But it was for her
But only until
The handle
Held strong
Because she had to carry
Her pail along
So a pail of sand
To you such a worthless thing
But to Sally
It was an important everything

Printed in the United States
by Baker & Taylor Publisher Services